This Handwriting Notebook Belongs To:

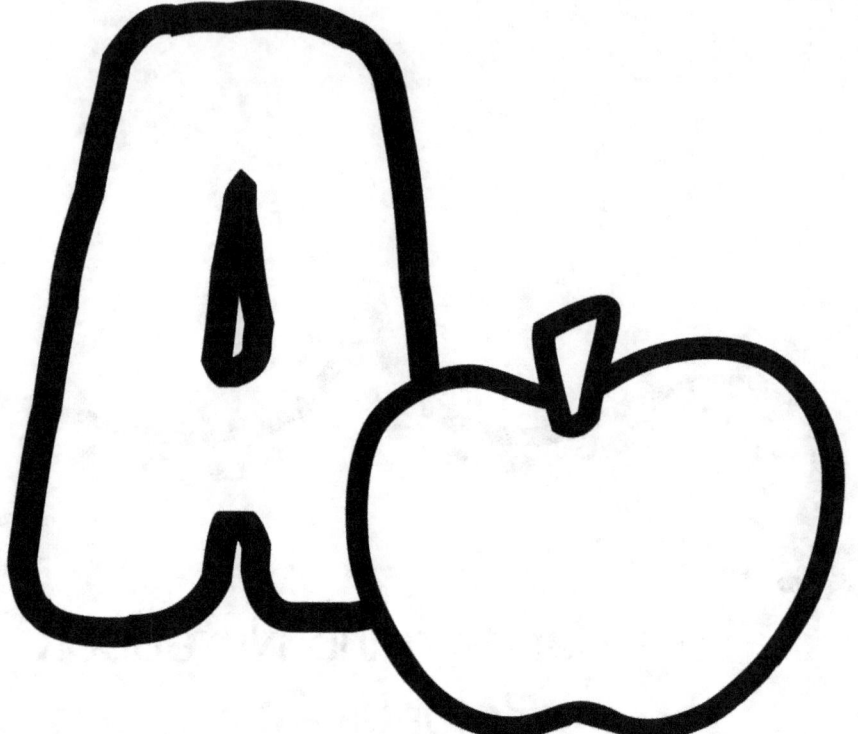

A

# A is For

B

# B is For

# C is For

# D is For

# E is For

# F is For

# G is For

# H is For

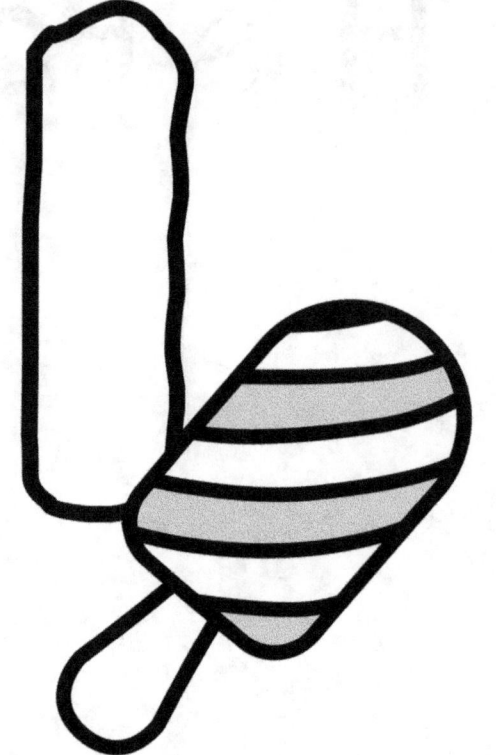

I

# I is For

J

# J is For

# K is For

L

# L is For

# M is For

# N is For

# O is For

P

# P is For

# Q is For

R

# R is For

s

# S is For

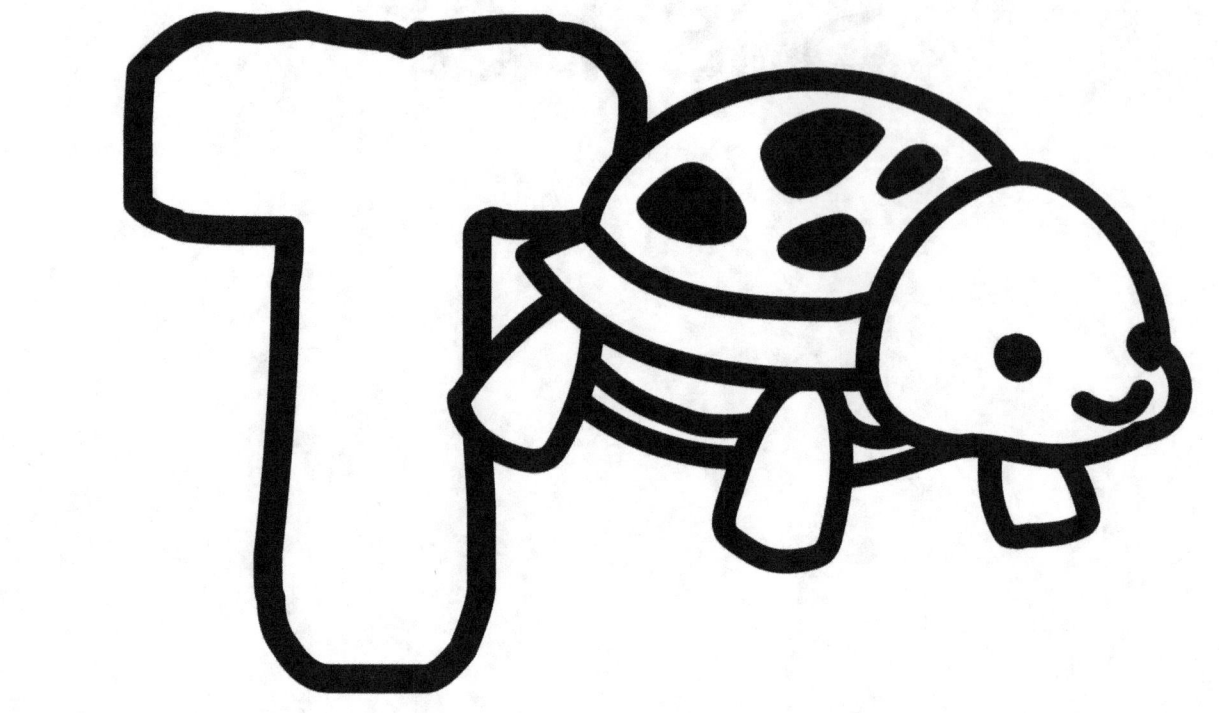

T

# T is For

# U is For

# V is For

# W is For

X

# X is For

Y

# Y is For

# Z is For

www.ingramcontent.com/pod-product-compliance
Lightning Source LLC
LaVergne TN
LVHW060155080526
838202LV00052B/4157